POEMS OF LIFE AND NATURE
Vol. 2

George William Ray, Jr.

ISBN Number 1-57087-048-9

Cover Picture by: Willard Gayheart
Production Design by: Robin Ober

Book Mark
PO Box 5044
Chapel Hill, NC 27515-4371

Manufactured in the United States of America
01 00 99 98 97 96   10 9 8 7 6 5 4 3 2 1

Joys of Life

The beauty of the flower
Sitting on the window sill
The beauty of some memories
As I sit and ponder still
The joy in my soul
As I dream and think of love
The treasure of the rainbow
As it arcs the sky above
The gladness I know
When I fill my place
The love of a child
So blessed with grace
These are truly the things
That make life good

Today you blessed me with a hug
And I really don't know why
But it was a very special thing to me
And almost made me cry
Perhaps you felt the need
For a little warmth or love
Or maybe you were sent to me
By our loving God above
To remind me that He cares
And to bring to me His love
When I was feeling a little blue.
Whatever was the reason
It was a sweet thing to do.
We all need from time to time
For someone else to care
And when we are feeling blue
for them their love to share
Know that today you found a friend
A faithful one and true
and anytime you have a problem
Know I'm here for you.

My Lovely One

You are so beautiful
My lovely one
As beautiful as the flowers
Touched by the morning sun
Even as sweet as the nectar
Of the early morning dew
These are the feelings
That I have for you.

Children In The Sand

Children play in the sand
With their tears and toys
And on the sands they leave their brand
Of castles and shells and other joys
They build their monuments by day
What a fantasy in their own right
As they dream of pirates and kings
But the sea takes them away by night
And fills the shore with other things.
Each day brings a new scene by light
A new crew of little ones
A different set of precious hands
Another bunch of sunburned buns
Play upon the sun scorched sands.

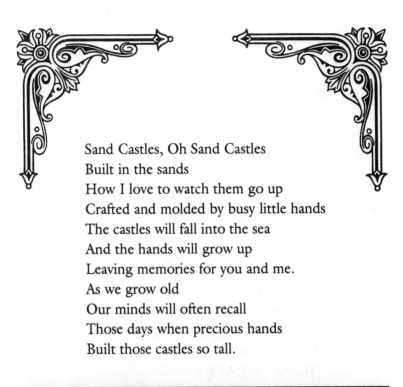

Sand Castles, Oh Sand Castles
Built in the sands
How I love to watch them go up
Crafted and molded by busy little hands
The castles will fall into the sea
And the hands will grow up
Leaving memories for you and me.
As we grow old
Our minds will often recall
Those days when precious hands
Built those castles so tall.

Sand Castles

Built of really gritty stuff
With spirals rising to the sky
Just one day is time enough
To build our towers up so high
For that night they will fall
Back into the raging surf
The surging giant will recall.

Let not your heart be troubled
But ever filled with love
For as sorrows fall upon you
There is always love from above
Count not the troubles
That you do find
But be ever blessed
With a joyful mind
Troubles and sorrows
Will take their toll
But smiles and joys
Will enhance the soul
So dwell upon the good
That life does give
And let your heart be never troubled
For as long as you live.

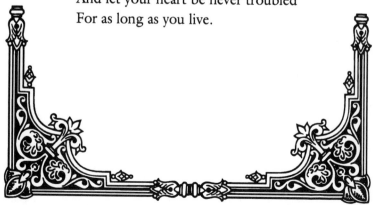

In a quiet hour
I rest my mind
And as I ponder
Old memories I find
Some are happy
And so good
Others I would forget
If I could.
But they are all part of me
And they help me better
The future to see
Bits and pieces I can't forsake
But life as a whole I must take.
I hope the joys and sorrows
That I have known
Will make me wiser
With future seeds to be sown
And that I will have made
This a better place
When it comes time
For me, my God to face.

Gifts From Above

I watched a little sparrow today
As he flitted and flew above
He didn't fly away, but up in a tree
And there he perched and sang a song of love.
And it was a beautiful thing to me
The most lovely sound I ever heard
This song that to me he sang
Such beauty to come from a little bird
Each note he sang rang so clear
This song he sang to me
Was so lovely falling upon my ear
And his music was given so free
The most beautiful things are not those we buy
But the gifts sent from God on high.

I treasure you as a friend
You are, I find, so neat
You give a friendly smile
And you are so sweet.
With a husky voice
You speak words of love
By you I am so blessed
You are a blessing from above
I hope my friend
You will always be
And through the years
Will treasure me.

Buddies

You say I'm your buddy
And that's so special to me
Cause without a buddy
What would this world be?
Just a place of sorrows and tears.
But with the help of a buddy
We can overcome our troubles and fears.
So if I'm your buddy
Then you're a buddy too
And know that I walk with you
In all that you do.

A Smile

Walking the roads of life
I sometimes feel a frown
Creeping across my face
And I try to not let it get me down
For soon I know a smile will come
Shining along my way
And I will share it with others
That I might brighten their day.
Then if that frown comes back
I hope they've kept the smile
And will pass it back to me
So I can plant it on my face
And happier I will be.

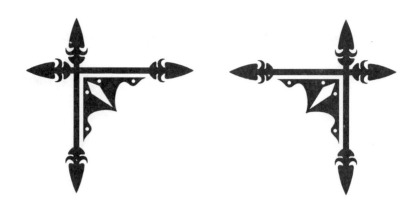

That pretty smile upon your face
So filled with joy and lovely grace
Must warm the hearts of everyone
Who is fortunate enough to see
The twinkle in your eyes
And that smile shared so free
I wish that smile may always be there
That all the world will be able to share
The joy that it brings to me
I pray that the heavens will you bless
And all your life be filled with happiness

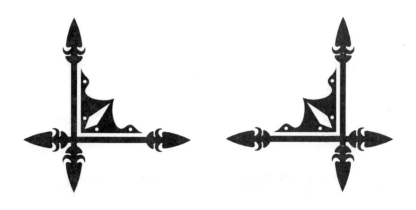

The Clouds

Ah, the clouds in the sky
I gaze at them, and,
How they do fly
Much as life, as we dream
Always in a hurry, always a rush
Few things are as they seem
And they both pass us by.

Life is like a river
An ever changing stream
Some days we live so vigorously
On others we just sit and dream
But the world waits not for us
As we drift along.
And we are better served
If we quickly find where we belong
For the world never waits for us.

A Cloudy Ride

Upon a fluffy cloud
I would like to take a ride
Then across the skies
I could up and glide
Across the mountain tops
To see the other side
But I can't fly that high
So here I must abide
And I guess I'll never get
To take a cloudy ride.

I watch the vulture
Crossing the sky
How he sails above the clouds
Up, up so very high
I wonder as I watch
Him sailing away
Where does he go,
Where will he be at end of day?

To A Precious One

Thank you my little friend
For all your love and kindness
Thank you for being my friend
And for all the ways me you bless
The tears fall from my eyes
When I think of you
You are so special to me
May you be blessed by all that I do.

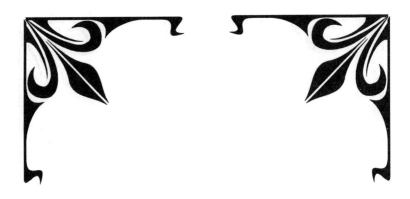

My darling dear little one
With freckles on your nose
How precious you are
And I don't suppose
I could ever make you know
How much you mean to me
But by doing little things
Perhaps I can make you see
That you are very, very special.

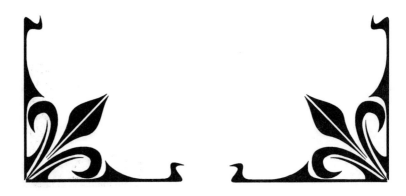

At First Light

As I walk the beach at first light
I find the treasure left by the waves last night
Seaweed and shells, treasure and junk
All kinds of things, but no pirate's trunk
I find the prints of someone who walked before me
And I know he saw the things I now see
A little fish dead on the beach
Crabs scurry away from my reach
There are ripples in the sand
Where the sea waters kissed the land.
This quiet hour of the early morn
As I watch a new day being born
Is a special time for me
And I thank God for letting me be
A part of this passing scene.

Love of the Sea

The sea, the sea is a place I love to be
I love its sand and shells and footprints
Oh how I love the sea!
I like the smell of the fish and crabs
And all the other smells I find
To just be near the sea is relaxing to my mind
The waters feel so good to me
When on just a whim
I strip away my clothes and take a swim
It is music to my soul to just sit upon the sand
And listen to the waves crashing upon the land
I love to watch the gulls spread their wings with a flair
And then dip and dive and sail through the air
Then the sunset, so beautiful as it sets upon the sea
The sea is truly a place where I love to be.

Rise Little Bird

Rise my little bird
And fly across the sky
Lift up your wings to heaven
And fly, fly, fly.
Above the fluffy clouds
Let your spirits soar
To seek what you can find
For you are shackled to earth nevermore
So spread those wings today
Be lifted up above
And as you fly away
May you be blessed with love.

Sometimes a bird can't stand its mate
And away it feels the need to fly
It might best serve its self to wait
And try to find the reason why
That love is lost and it is so sad
And has no joy and happiness.
Perhaps it's the cause for love to turn so bad
It may have never shown finesse
But birds will fly away in haste
And put all caution to the wind
Yes, in this rush they make waste
Of all chance for their hearts to mend.
They fly away to other places
In their search for newer faces
Oh fly away my little bird
And see what you can find
You don't listen to my spoken word
And you have no peace of mind
Therefore you feel the need to fly
You would better spend your time in thought
And ponder the things that bring sorrow
But you have no time for thought in your angry mad
So fly away my little bird, I wish the best for you
May you never more be hurt and sad.
I wish you the best in all that you do.

Lonesome Traveler

I'm just a lonesome traveler
Wandering along life's way
Seeking joy and happiness
And a little love each day
I pray the spirits will guide me
As I seek the path that is true
And by way of that guidance
May I bring some joy to you.

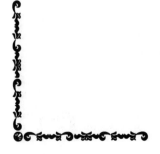

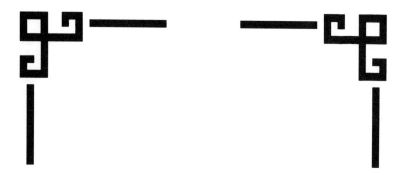

How does it feel
To cause hurt without care
I ask you truly
Because I've never been there
Through hurts and sorrows
I've felt the pain
As others pricked my feelings
For their own gain
But in my hurt and my sorrow
I cannot do the same
For from the depths of my soul I love
I cannot play that hurting game.

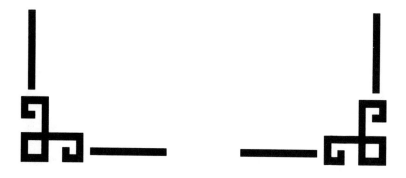

Through eyes filled with
Tear stained passion
I watched my whole world cry
And in my own hurting fashion
I pondered and wondered why
That some hurt others
And without a care
Don't they know the pain they cause
Or have they never been there
Have they no compassion or love
Possess they no feelings true
Are they really that cold and heartless
Or know they not, what they do.

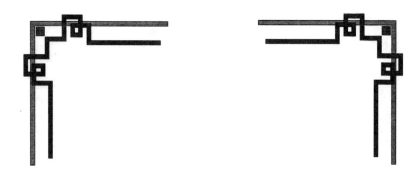

Thank you Jesus for the joy you bring
Thank you for your love and everything
You, my life have truly blessed
Though sins I have confessed
I can feel your presence everywhere
And where I am I know you are there
Everywhere your blessings I see
As I am blessed, may others be blessed by me
Hold me and guide me by your hand
Help me to spread joy throughout the land.
For your will I try to do
Help me truly to live for you.

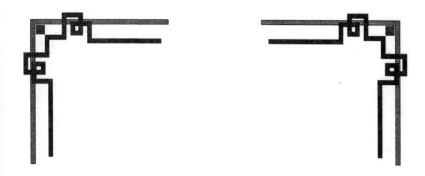

Faith

My trust is in Jesus, I have no fear
He blesses me with his love
And fills my heart with cheer
As I fly across the skies
How close to Him I feel
Held by binding Christian ties
I know His love is real.
I look down upon the earth this Christmas morn
And thinking of His great worth
I thank God that He was born.

*This poem was written on a Christmas morning as the
author sat in a plane at 30,000 feet altitude.*

As you are in labor
And do spend this day
May you be so blessed
By the little one on the way
There is nothing so sweet
As a little child
They are so endearing
Sometimes so meek and mild.
I know much joy
To you he will bring
Though sometimes trying
With a fit he'll fling
Just remember, not a castaway toy
You bring into the world
A dear sweet little girl or boy.

Hardheaded and stubborn
A few stand apart
And yes, quite often
Wind up with a broken heart
Still they cannot forsake
The principles and values
In which they believe
Even though to do so sometimes
Would their emotions relieve
To give in and these things forsake
Would invite Satan
Their souls to take.

Many a time when the fickle finger of fate
Stops and points itself at you
You'll find yourself examining your every trait
And wondering what you should do.
Why me, you may cry out
As life's troubles upon you sink
You may well have reason to doubt,
This you may often think.
And you may feel you are lost for sure
But you must never give in
No matter how bad, you can endure.
Just keep on fighting through thick and thin
For as you fight, you become stronger
And you can find the way
No matter how fierce the battle
To fight a little longer
And then you'll win some day.

Life is not easy
For one with a true spirit
And a kind and loving heart
For as they try to bring joy
They will be cursed by others
Who lie and do their cheating part.
Ah, the sorrows we find
As we pass along life's way
Snares and tears are ours
We'll find some each day
But then again
There are joys to be found
And we must search them out.
On the good things of life
We must ponder and dwell
That our hearts and souls may be abound
With the fulfillment that comes
From love.

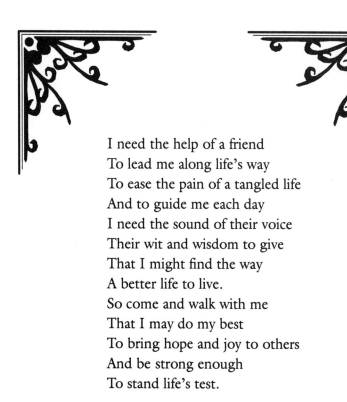

I need the help of a friend
To lead me along life's way
To ease the pain of a tangled life
And to guide me each day
I need the sound of their voice
Their wit and wisdom to give
That I might find the way
A better life to live.
So come and walk with me
That I may do my best
To bring hope and joy to others
And be strong enough
To stand life's test.

The author has often sat on his boat and written down thoughts that came to mind, often writing these down in the pages of a previous book of poems. The boat sank during the night of Hurricane Fran, 1996 and remained under water for ten days. When the boat was refloated, the author searched for and found the book with his poems written in its pages and which was the only copy. This poem was among them.

As I watched the morning light
Come creeping across the hills so bright
And shadows falling away
I wondered what this day would bring
Good or bad, what kind of thing
And I really wondered too
If it would be good or bad
Would it make me unhappy or glad.
Ah the intrigue of a new day breaking
T'is truly a thing of mystery
If one does ponder upon it you see
And I suppose it's really best
That I not know what bring it may
So I will strive harder to make it go my way.

Yon mountain beckons to me
Even as a gull would be called to the sea
Come climb my spirals to the top
To me it calls out
And I believe I could without doubt.
I wonder what would lie between here and there
And I would climb that mountain top on a dare
How I wonder what's on the other side of that hill
And someday I'll climb it, I know I will
Oh I know it would be simpler to drive to the other side
And I might even enjoy the ride.
But it just wouldn't be the same with the challenge gone
So someday I'll just climb that hill, if I have to go alone
And when I reach the top and look over the side
I'll be glad that I didn't just take the ride
And happy I will be
Because I did it just for me.

Close your eyes my friend
And let your spirits soar
Let the timeless mystics send
Joy, peace, happiness, love and more
Of the things that fulfillment brings
Let your soul be filled with love
As your every emotion sings
Know your blessings from above
Feel the stillness of your quiet hour
And know the peace that surrounds
As you direct your inner power
And feel the surge that abounds
Be lifted from this place
Into another world
And may you be blessed with a happier face
Upon your return.

Thanks

As I stand upon the sands
And gaze out to sea
My mind dreams of other lands
Yet here I am glad to be
I'm thankful for life
And all the joys it holds
I'm thankful for love
As in our lives it unfolds
I'm glad for all the good things
And I'll deal with the bad
For a combo of both life brings
And life is too short to be sad.

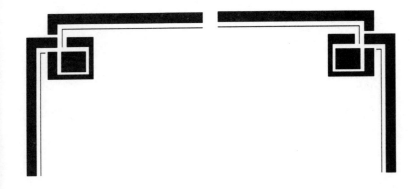

Friends

Across the span of your life
Observing you will find
Many, that your friends claim to be
Seek only to toy with your mind
They seek for their own gain
And they will spread no sunshine
But only sorrow and clouds of rain.
So be wary while searching for friends
And be careful of the ones you take
By the true ones be blessed
The others your heart will break.

Blue Eyes

Ah my pretty one
With eyes so blue
You are so beautiful
One could easily fall for you
Here's praying you are as lovely
Inside as you are on the out
If that be the fact
You are cherishable without a doubt.

Passions

Passions arise my love
When I think of you, you on my mind
Are you truly sent from above
Or in your thoughts do deceit you find
Should I accept you as right
Or in my mixed emotions
Should I run in fright?
I would drink you as one of life's potions
Yes, as a nectar so sweet
And hope in true love
We were intended to meet
These my mysteries I cannot solve
For as I dream of you
Around you my emotions revolve.
I feel I must accept love
While love is here
That I be not alone
And if someday it goes,
It will just be gone.

I look upon your face
And my heart is quickened
By the beauty that I see
Even as love soars there
And fills my life
With the joys of passion
That are new to me.
What are these feelings
That take over my being
And blind my eyes
To the dangers that lurk
Just ahead in my life?
What is this thing
That hides from me
Your every flaw and fault,
And keeps me from seeing
The heartbreak that lies ahead?
Love, you fickle thing.

Take not a life
Not even your own
But share a gift of love
Be not sad
Not even a little
Enjoy your blessings from above

Seek the good
Give what you can
Enjoy each day.
Let not your heart be troubled
As you travel along life's way.

Let not your soul be troubled
God has a place for you
Just believe in Jesus
And He will see you through
As you spend your youth
And often in troubles stand
Just trust in Jesus
God will lead you by His hand
He will be with you
Through the mid age years
And if you trust in Him
He will calm your fears
Then when you approach
The years of old
Fear not my friend
But face them strong and bold
For God has a plan for you
And if you trust in Him
He will see you through.

Jesus came and lived
That He might save us from sin
That we might be saved from eternal loss
He gave Himself
That we might be cleansed
That's why He died upon the cross
T'is a wondrous life He does give
And great joys He will bring
If His will we choose to live
And will His great praises sing.
Oh joy, oh joy to my soul
Let me live my life each day
That my name might be put
Forever in heaven's scroll
And let me be guided along life's way
By His great and wondrous love
Let me live my life for him,
And when I die, may I awake above.

Thank you Father for sending your Son
So many years ago He came
Even as you said it would be done
A Savior indeed sent from above
He came to a manager
And He came to bring your love
To a world so filled with sin
He came, yes He came
That we might have a way to enter in
Into the grace of His saving power
That we might be ready
For we know not the day or hour
When we will be called home.
But we can be saved by His grace
So that our souls may never more roam.

Springtime burst abloom today
With sunshine everywhere
And the simmering rays
Warm the depths of me 'eart
T'is indeed an experience I have craved
All the long winter through
And now t'is finally 'ere
I find no sorrow now
But filled with joy I am
For t'is my time of the year.
Oh joy, joy to my soul
For the chill winds, no longer
Do they blow across the land
And the cold foggy mornings
Gone they are from the dell.
Aye for a season I know
The chill tongue of winter
Is melted away and gone.

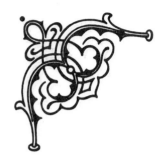
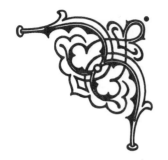

Spring

I smell the honeysuckle
Its scent wafting in the morning air
I see the doves wing past me in a pair
The robins are pulling their food from the ground
And I can feel spring all around
The grass is so nice and green
And I watch the birds as their feathers they preen
And the morning air is filled with their songs
As they gather together in throngs
I must say, to me, spring does appear
To be the best time of the year.

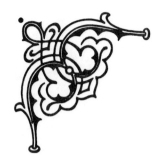
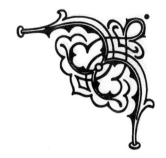

I watch a little brown leaf flutter
As it answers nature's call
And know that soon all its cousins
Will float to the ground
For it's that time of year, yes it's fall.
Soon the leaves will be blown into many a pile
Their colors all mixed in a brilliant hue
By the chill wind that blows all the while
And gives me a feeling of loneliness so blue
Fast on its heels, winter is sure to come.
I dread all its dampness and cold,
Though the thought brings happiness to some.
I will face the coming season without fear
For as the cold surrounds us
I know spring will soon be here.

Anguish

You cried out in your anguished pain
I could feel your hurt and sorrow
And those tear drops, they fell like rain
But there was no comfort I could give
For too deep was my own anguish
And through it all we each had to live
We had to look for solace in our own way
As we searched our souls for peace
And prayed for a better day.

My emotions have crossed
A wide and stormy sea
And as I crossed that angry space
No one could hear my plea
My very soul cried out
As I fought the storm
But no one could hear my shout
How I cried for a helping hand
Engulfed by the rolling waves
But there was no help as I sought the land
No help no help, none for me
As I fought the tempest
And swam an angry sea
No help could I find
Until I calmed my inner soul
By the strength of my own mind
Now the storms have passed away
And I find a blessed peace
As I live each day.

My Sinking Sun

Ah my love, I'm sinking fast
I've run my race, I can not last
My life is almost done
The final hour for me has come
The chariots from heaven I can see
My time has come, my love, for me
To leave this old place
For my heavenly home
Where I will see my Savior's face,
Weep not for me, my love
Waste not your tears
For I will arise to that land above
Though you will be alone
When I am gone
May you be blest and a joyful one
As I fade away in my sinking sun.

Freedom

Oh joy, oh joy is mine
For great joy I find
In the peace that is given to me
Because I am set free.
Free in body, mind, and soul
I have no sorrows to take their toll
All my burdens are lifted away
And joy and peace are mine today
My emotions sail to heights unknown
Because of the joys that to me are shown
I dare not ask for anything more
For I remember the burdens of before
And now just peace and joy I see
How great it is to be free.

The Sentinel

Yon lonely sentinel
Is but an old oak tree
Its heart has become doty
Much perhaps like me
Yet it stands alone
Above all the rest
Though broken and scored
It has stood the test.
Someday I know
That it must fall
Such is a part of life
Fate, it awaits us all.

The Sand Crab

The sand crab is a creepy little thing
Building a home in the ground
As load after load of sand, out he brings
Then he hides in his hole
There in the darkness
Much like a mole.
He creeps to the top right after dark
But when he sees you coming
He scurries away like a lark.
He is not likely to be caught
For to be ever alert
By nature he is taught
But if you walk the beach at night
You will see him scurry away
If you are really quick of sight.

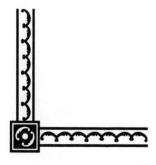

Sands of Time

I walk across the sands
That my younger feet did trod
But it is not the same
Though it be the same old sod
Truly we cannot go back
To the same old places
Locations may be the same
But there are ever new faces
We cannot turn back time
Even should we try
The world moves on
We are born, we live, we die.

Memories

Saddened are my emotions
As I survey the depths
And the memories of my mind
The things I once so loved
They are no longer mine
Both good times and sorrows
These I do forever recall
The good times with such sweetness
And the sorrows with gall
New faces I see all around
And where they stand and walk
New tracks upon the ground.
And I know as I look back
I too, will become a memory.

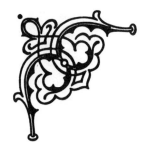
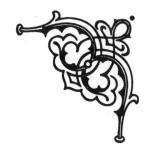

Deep Waters

Along the banks of deep waters
I've walked the slippery path
And by the burdens of this life
Been pulled ever nearer
To the edge of that abyss
Into which I could have
So easily slipped and fallen
Oh so closely at times
I've trod that narrow way
And known the darkness
Of the deepening shadows
That beckoned me ever closer.
And only by narrow margin
Have I been called away
By the voice of a friend
That gave me the strength
To hold on to the threads
That bound me to life.

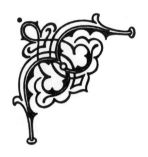
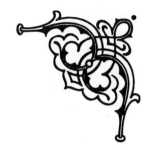

My Anchor*

To you my friend
I do bid thanks
For being the anchor
That has kept me from
Drifting into the places
Where treacherous waters
Would have ripped apart
The very seams and timbers
Which bind me together.
Yes, thanks to you,
For holding me steady
In the swirling current
Of the main stream
Where life flows so fast.

Oh love you fickle thing
I've known your joys
And I've felt your sting
How often I've been
A patron of your game.
You bring such gladness to a heart
When you're on one's side
And yet the sorrows you impart
When you show your hurting traits
By you I've been so blessed
Then you turned against me
And I became so stressed
Oh love you fickle one
I find you not a trusted friend.

We walk through the shadows
Of an ever changing world
As we travel the paths of life
Sometimes so blessed of fortune
And yet evil ever stalks us.
There is no escape my friend
From this thing called fate.
Yes indeed it does
Await for us one and all
Sometimes pouring out its blessings
And then sometimes snatching them away
Never can we be sure
What may await for us
Until we walk the last path
And take the final step.

Around and around a pat of mud
I watch your fingers fly
As you sit and play
And make a muddy pie
What a joyful sight
To watch a little one
Sitting in a puddle of mud
Having so much fun.

In your moment of passion
You peaked my interest
With your game of tease
But I doubt your sincerity
I believe you never intended
To bring joy or to please
For as I muse over your actions
Your purpose, I tend to find
Is just a game you seek
To play with my mind
And so you've caused a little hurt
When you flirted without care
But I wish you no sorrow
May you be blessed
With love everywhere.

Crunch, crunch my boots
Squeak across the snow
Here and there I see tracks
And I wonder where they go
All the world seems still
And covered in glossy white
Bathed in a blanket of snowy cold
And it all fell during the night.

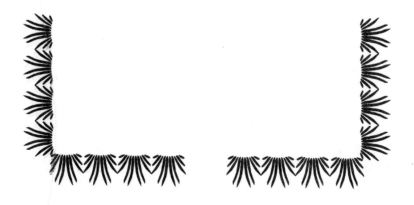

Blessings From Above

I'm so happy this morning
I'm so blessed with love
Showers of blessing are upon me
They fall down from above.

How great is His mercy
How great is His love
How wondrous those blessings
He showers from above.

There are no tethers
My soul knows no bounds
My life is so wondrous
His love my soul surrounds.

Chorus:
I'm blessed by His mercy
I'm blessed by His love
He pours showers upon me
From the heavens above.